CW00428053

tained Pages

"MILE by MILE"

by

S. N. PIKE, M.B.E.

WATERLOO EDITION
SOUTHERN RAILWAY

A book of some 10,000 words and 27 maps, describing in detail the main line Railway between London and Towns of the South and South-West; showing :—

- GRADIENTS
- MILEAGES
- SPEEDS
- JUNCTIONS
- VIADUCTS
- TUNNELS
- RIVERS and
- ROADS

with an account of features of interest and beauty to be seen from the train.

A facsimile reprint by

Silver Link Publishing Ltd
Unit 5, Home Farm Close, Church Street,
Wadenhoe, Peterborough PE8 5TE

© Nick Dodson 1988

Originally published in 1947 by Stuart N. Pike, Worthing
Facsimile edition first published in December 1988
by Silver Link Publishing Ltd
Reprinted March 1993

British Library Cataloguing in Publication Data

Pike, S. N. (Stuart N)
Travelling on the Southern railway: the journey
mile by mile. – Waterloo edition
I. Title
385.0941

ISBN 0 947971 88 2

Printed and bound in Great Britain

The
Best Railway Book
ever published

This book has been described as the " Best Railway Book ever published." Whether or no it deserves this description is left to the purchaser. Certainly the wealth of detail here collected must give it a high place amongst books about travelling by rail.

The route is through 149 Stations on the Southern Railway, covering the main line between London and the South and South-west. Each page contains a description of the countryside and what is to be seen of interest on that Section. On the right side of each page is data dear to the heart of the railway enthusiast. Gradients, bridges, viaducts and their height, tunnels and their length, junctions, cuttings, speeds, and approximate running times between Stations.

No less than 60 rivers and streams are encountered and named.

It is intended that the book be read whilst actually in the train. It may be commenced at any point of the journey. A glance at the name of the Station just passed, a reference to the Index, and what will be seen between there and the next Station is described. Not only what will be seen, but approximately how long it will take to reach that next Station and at what speed, and on what degree of gradient the train will be either climbing up, or coasting down at that moment.

Small figures indicate the height of the line and that of the surrounding country above sea level, enabling the traveller to anticipate his arrival at a valley, or otherwise. The position of all bridges—even foot bridges—over the line is indicated to enable features mentioned in the commentary to be the more easily pinpointed. For the same reason the position of grid cables near or crossing the line is given.

A gradient of 1 : 80 means that for every 80 yards or feet travelled the line has risen or fallen by one yard or one foot, as indicated on the right of each page.

To view the countryside as described by the Author, travellers towards the coast should sit facing the engine; those travelling towards London, with their backs to the engine.

Rivers we meet

Anton
Avon (Wilts.)
Avon (Hants.)
Axe

Basingstoke Canal
Batts Brook
Beaulieu
Blackwater
Bourne
Bray
Burn

Clyst
Corfe
Creedy
Culm
Culvery

Dalch

East Okement
Ems
Exe

Frome

Hogsmill

Itchen

Lew
Little Dart
Lodden
Loddon
Lumburn
Lyd
Lyde
Lymington
Lynher

Mole
Mude

Nadder

Okement
Otter

Parrett

Rother

Sem
Sid
Sherford
Stour (Dorset)
Stour (Hants.)

Tale
Tamar
Tavy
Taw
Test
Thames
Tilmore
Trent (Dorset)

Umborne

Walkham
Wandle
West Okement
Wey (Dorset)
Wey (Surrey)
Wylye

Yeo

Counties

London
Surrey
Sussex
Hampshire

Wiltshire
Dorsetshire
Somersetshire
Devonshire

4

Index to Stations

5

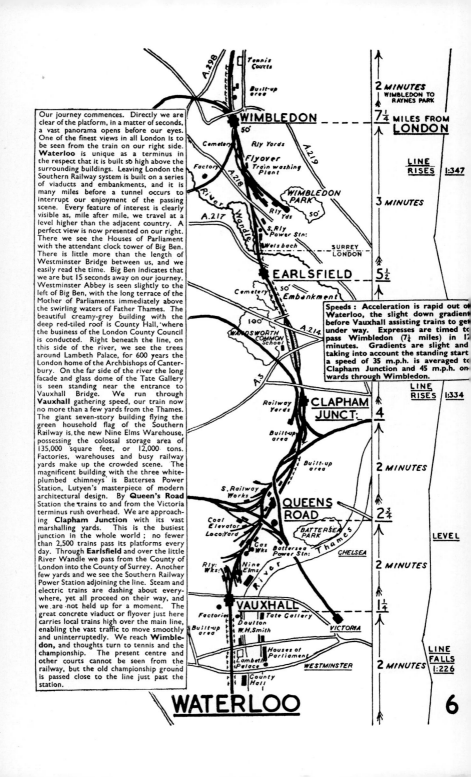

Our journey commences. Directly we are clear of the platform, in a matter of seconds, a vast panorama opens before our eyes. One of the finest views in all London is to be seen from the train on our right side. **Waterloo** is unique as a terminus in the respect that it is built so high above the surrounding buildings. Leaving London the Southern Railway system is built on a series of viaducts and embankments, and it is many miles before a tunnel occurs to interrupt our enjoyment of the passing scene. Every feature of interest is clearly visible as, mile after mile, we travel at a level higher than the adjacent country. A perfect view is now presented on our right. There we see the Houses of Parliament with the attendant clock tower of Big Ben. There is little more than the length of Westminster Bridge between us, and we easily read the time. Big Ben indicates that we are but 15 seconds away on our journey. Westminster Abbey is seen slightly to the left of Big Ben, with the long terrace of the Mother of Parliaments immediately above the swirling waters of Father Thames. The beautiful creamy-grey building with the deep red-tiled roof is County Hall, where the business of the London County Council is conducted. Right beneath the line, on this side of the river, we see the trees around Lambeth Palace, for 600 years the London home of the Archbishops of Canterbury. On the far side of the river the long facade and glass dome of the Tate Gallery is seen standing near the entrance to Vauxhall Bridge. We run through **Vauxhall** gathering speed, our train now no more than a few yards from the Thames. The giant seven-story building flying the green household flag of the Southern Railway is, the new Nine Elms Warehouse, possessing the colossal storage area of 135,000 square feet, or 12,000 tons. Factories, warehouses and busy railway yards make up the crowded scene. The magnificent building with the three white-plumbed chimneys is Battersea Power Station, Lutyen's masterpiece of modern architectural design. By **Queen's Road** Station the trains to and from the Victoria terminus rush overhead. We are approaching **Clapham Junction** with its vast marshalling yards. This is the busiest junction in the whole world; no fewer than 2,500 trains pass its platforms every day. Through **Earlsfield** and over the little River Wandle we pass from the County of London into the County of Surrey. Another few yards and we see the Southern Railway Power Station adjoining the line. Steam and electric trains are dashing about everywhere, yet all proceed on their way, and we are not held up for a moment. The great concrete viaduct or flyover just here carries local trains high over the main line, enabling the vast traffic to move smoothly and uninterruptedly. We reach **Wimbledon**, and thoughts turn to tennis and the championship. The present centre and other courts cannot be seen from the railway, but the old championship ground is passed close to the line just past the station.

Speeds: Acceleration is rapid out of Waterloo, the slight down gradient before Vauxhall assisting trains to get under way. Expresses are timed to pass Wimbledon (7¼ miles) in 12 minutes. Gradients are slight and taking into account the standing start a speed of 35 m.p.h. is averaged to Clapham Junction and 45 m.p.h. onwards through Wimbledon.

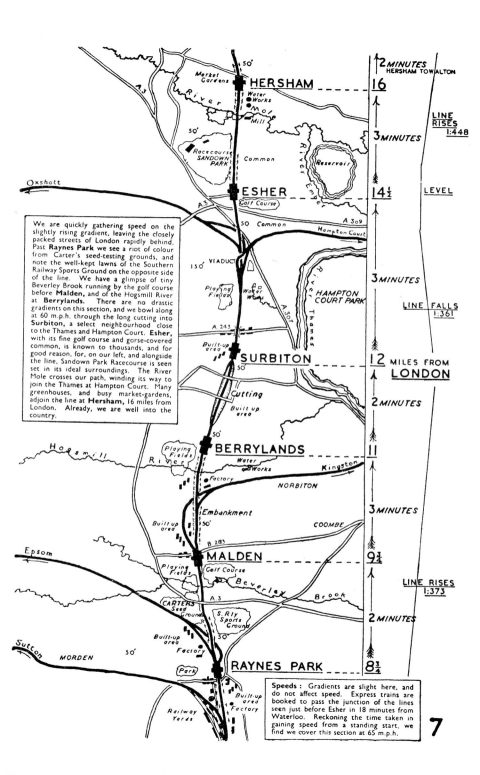

We are quickly gathering speed on the slightly rising gradient, leaving the closely packed streets of London rapidly behind. Past **Raynes Park** we see a riot of colour from Carter's seed-testing grounds, and note the well-kept lawns of the Southern Railway Sports Ground on the opposite side of the line. We have a glimpse of tiny Beverley Brook running by the golf course before **Malden**, and of the Hogsmill River at **Berrylands.** There are no drastic gradients on this section, and we bowl along at 60 m.p.h. through the long cutting into **Surbiton**, a select neighbourhood close to the Thames and Hampton Court. **Esher**, with its fine golf course and gorse-covered common, is known to thousands, and for good reason, for, on our left, and alongside the line, Sandown Park Racecourse is seen set in its ideal surroundings. The River Mole crosses our path, winding its way to join the Thames at Hampton Court. Many greenhouses, and busy market-gardens, adjoin the line at **Hersham**, 16 miles from London. Already, we are well into the country.

Speeds : Gradients are slight here, and do not affect speed. Express trains are booked to pass the junction of the lines seen just before Esher in 18 minutes from Waterloo. Reckoning the time taken in gaining speed from a standing start, we find we cover this section at 65 m.p.h.

7

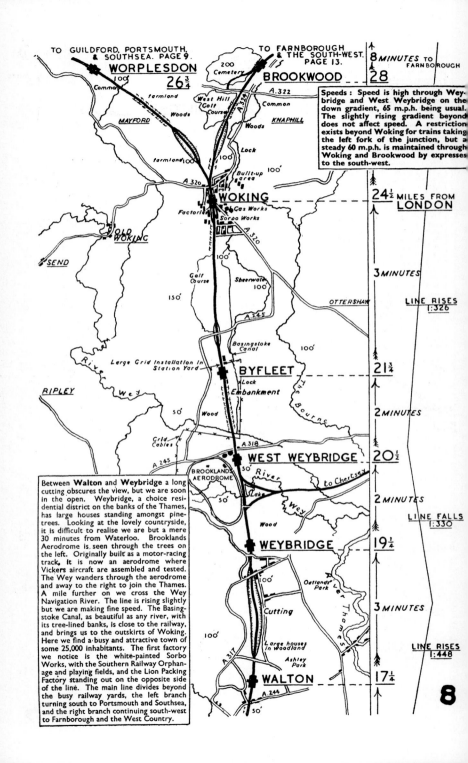

WORPLESDON 26¾

BROOKWOOD 8 MINUTES TO FARNBOROUGH — 28

Speeds : Speed is high through Weybridge and West Weybridge on the down gradient, 65 m.p.h. being usual. The slightly rising gradient beyond does not affect speed. A restriction exists beyond Woking for trains taking the left fork of the junction, but a steady 60 m.p.h. is maintained through Woking and Brookwood by expresses to the south-west.

WOKING — 24½ MILES FROM **LONDON**

3 MINUTES · LINE RISES 1:326

BYFLEET — 21¾

2 MINUTES

WEST WEYBRIDGE — 20½

2 MINUTES · LINE FALLS 1:330

WEYBRIDGE — 19¼

3 MINUTES · LINE RISES 1:448

WALTON — 17¼

Between **Walton** and **Weybridge** a long cutting obscures the view, but we are soon in the open. Weybridge, a choice residential district on the banks of the Thames, has large houses standing amongst pine-trees. Looking at the lovely countryside, it is difficult to realise we are but a mere 30 minutes from Waterloo. Brooklands Aerodrome is seen through the trees on the left. Originally built as a motor-racing track, it is now an aerodrome where Vickers aircraft are assembled and tested. The Wey wanders through the aerodrome and away to the right to join the Thames. A mile further on we cross the Wey Navigation River. The line is rising slightly but we are making fine speed. The Basingstoke Canal, as beautiful as any river, with its tree-lined banks, is close to the railway, and brings us to the outskirts of Woking. Here we find a busy and attractive town of some 25,000 inhabitants. The first factory we notice is the white-painted Sorbo Works, with the Southern Railway Orphanage and playing fields, and the Lion Packing Factory standing out on the opposite side of the line. The main line divides beyond the busy railway yards, the left branch turning south to Portsmouth and Southsea, and the right branch continuing south-west to Farnborough and the West Country.

8

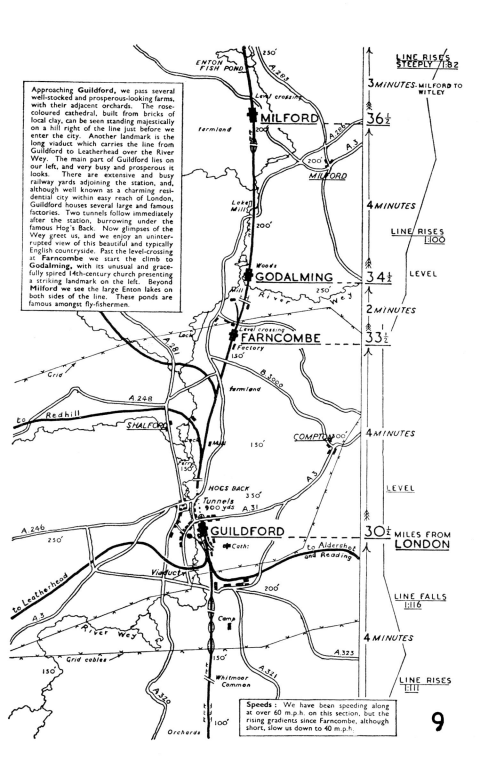

ENTON FISH POND

250'
A 283
Level crossing

MILFORD — — $36\frac{1}{2}$

farmland
200'
A 286
A 3

200'
MILFORD

Lake
Mill
200'

Woods
GODALMING — — $34\frac{1}{2}$

Mill
River Wey
250'

Loch

Level crossing
FARNCOMBE - - - $33\frac{1}{2}$
Factory
150'

B 3000

A 281

Grid

farmland

A 248

to Redhill

SHALFORD
MILL
150'

Mill
150'

COMPTON 100'

A 3

150'

HOGS BACK
350'
Tunnels
900 yds
A 31

A 246
250'

GUILDFORD — — $30\frac{1}{2}$
Cath:
to Aldershot and Reading

Viaduct

to Leatherhead

A 3
River Wey
Camp
200'

Grid cables

150'

150'
Whitmoor Common

A 320
100'

A 323
A 321

Orchards

LINE RISES STEEPLY 1:82

3 MINUTES - MILFORD TO WITLEY

4 MINUTES

LINE RISES 1:100

LEVEL

2 MINUTES

4 MINUTES

LEVEL

MILES FROM **LONDON**

LINE FALLS 1:116

4 MINUTES

LINE RISES 1:111

Approaching **Guildford**, we pass several well-stocked and prosperous-looking farms, with their adjacent orchards. The rose-coloured cathedral, built from bricks of local clay, can be seen standing majestically on a hill right of the line just before we enter the city. Another landmark is the long viaduct which carries the line from Guildford to Leatherhead over the River Wey. The main part of Guildford lies on our left, and very busy and prosperous it looks. There are extensive and busy railway yards adjoining the station, and, although well known as a charming residential city within easy reach of London, Guildford houses several large and famous factories. Two tunnels follow immediately after the station, burrowing under the famous Hog's Back. Now glimpses of the Wey greet us, and we enjoy an uninterrupted view of this beautiful and typically English countryside. Past the level-crossing at **Farncombe** we start the climb to **Godalming**, with its unusual and gracefully spired 14th-century church presenting a striking landmark on the left. Beyond **Milford** we see the large Enton lakes on both sides of the line. These ponds are famous amongst fly-fishermen.

Speeds : We have been speeding along at over 60 m.p.h. on this section, but the rising gradients since Farncombe, although short, slow us down to 40 m.p.h.

9

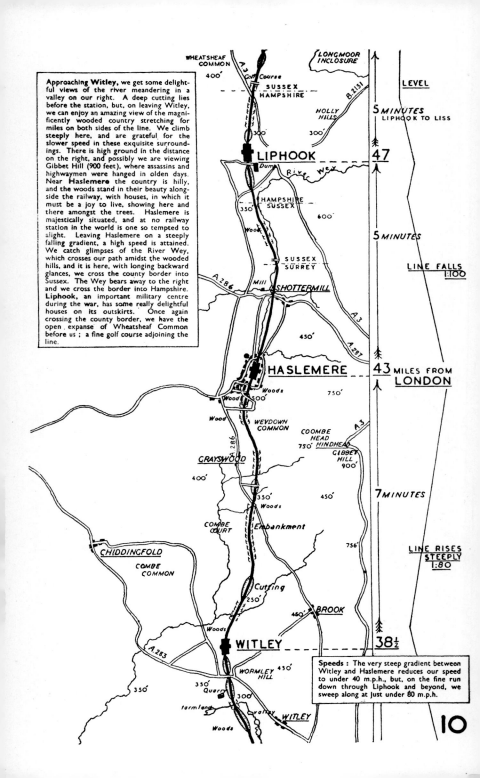

Approaching **Witley**, we get some delightful views of the river meandering in a valley on our right. A deep cutting lies before the station, but, on leaving Witley, we can enjoy an amazing view of the magnificently wooded country stretching for miles on both sides of the line. We climb steeply here, and are grateful for the slower speed in these exquisite surroundings. There is high ground in the distance on the right, and possibly we are viewing Gibbet Hill (900 feet), where assassins and highwaymen were hanged in olden days. Near **Haslemere** the country is hilly, and the woods stand in their beauty alongside the railway, with houses, in which it must be a joy to live, showing here and there amongst the trees. Haslemere is majestically situated, and at no railway station in the world is one so tempted to alight. Leaving Haslemere on a steeply falling gradient, a high speed is attained. We catch glimpses of the River Wey, which crosses our path amidst the wooded hills, and it is here, with longing backward glances, we cross the county border into Sussex. The Wey bears away to the right and we cross the border into Hampshire. Liphook, an important military centre during the war, has some really delightful houses on its outskirts. Once again crossing the county border, we have the open expanse of Wheatsheaf Common before us ; a fine golf course adjoining the line.

WHEATSHEAF COMMON
400'
LONGMOOR INCLOSURE

LEVEL

Golf Course

SUSSEX
HAMPSHIRE

5 MINUTES
LIPHOOK TO LISS

HOLLY HILLS
300'
300'

LIPHOOK
47

Dump
River Wey

HAMPSHIRE
SUSSEX
350'
600'
Woods

5 MINUTES

LINE FALLS
1:100

A 286
Mill
SUSSEX
SURREY
SHOTTERMILL

A 3

450'
A 287

HASLEMERE
43 MILES FROM LONDON

Woods
Wood 500'
Wood
WEYDOWN COMMON
750'

COOMBE HEAD
HINDHEAD
750'
A 3

GIBBET HILL
900'

GRAYSWOOD
400'
A 286

350'
Woods
450'

7 MINUTES

COMBE COURT
Embankment

756'

LINE RISES STEEPLY
1:80

CHIDDINGFOLD
COMBE COMMON

Cutting
250'

450'
BROOK

Woods
A 283

WITLEY
38½

WORMLEY HILL
450'

350'
350'
Quarry
300'
farmland
Valley **WITLEY**
Woods

Speeds : The very steep gradient between Witley and Haslemere reduces our speed to under 40 m.p.h., but, on the fine run down through Liphook and beyond, we sweep along at just under 80 m.p.h.

10

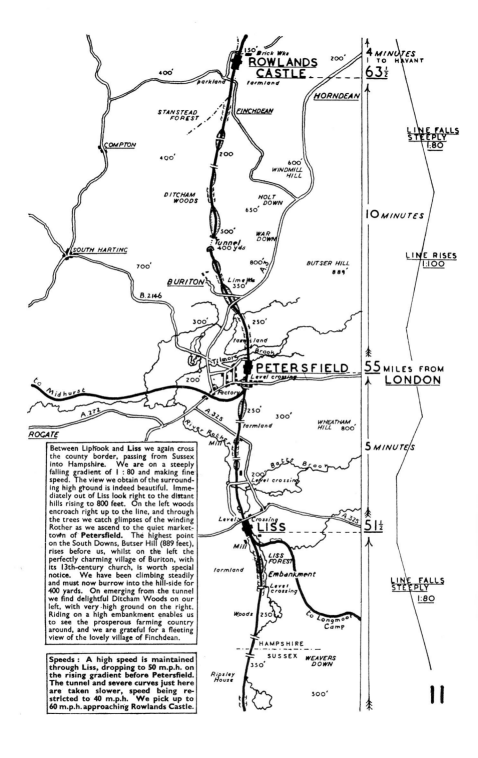

Between Liphook and **Liss** we again cross the county border, passing from Sussex into Hampshire. We are on a steeply falling gradient of 1 : 80 and making fine speed. The view we obtain of the surrounding high ground is indeed beautiful. Immediately out of Liss look right to the distant hills rising to 800 feet. On the left woods encroach right up to the line, and through the trees we catch glimpses of the winding Rother as we ascend to the quiet market-town of **Petersfield**. The highest point on the South Downs, Butser Hill (889 feet), rises before us, whilst on the left the perfectly charming village of Buriton, with its 13th-century church, is worth special notice. We have been climbing steadily and must now burrow into the hill-side for 400 yards. On emerging from the tunnel we find delightful Ditcham Woods on our left, with very high ground on the right. Riding on a high embankment enables us to see the prosperous farming country around, and we are grateful for a fleeting view of the lovely village of Finchdean.

Speeds : A high speed is maintained through Liss, dropping to 50 m.p.h. on the rising gradient before Petersfield. The tunnel and severe curves just here are taken slower, speed being restricted to 40 m.p.h. We pick up to 60 m.p.h. approaching Rowlands Castle.

ENGLISH CHANNEL

Within 15 minutes we shall have reached the sea. The hills are being left behind, and we are now running through flat farmland where numerous cattle peacefully graze. As we approach the old market town of **Havant**, we see the railway from Chichester approaching the junction. Our speed is now very slow as we take the curve into the station. The line turns sharply to the west here and we proceed slowly over the level crossings to Bedhampton Halt, where, looking left, we have our first view of the sea in Langstone Harbour, with Hayling Island in the distance. Looking right we see the line of disused forts on Ports Down, originally built to defend the harbour, with numerous well-sited houses on the lower slopes of the Downs. Through marshland we cross the junction of the line to Southampton, pass over the creek and on to **Hilsea Halt**. A large aerodrome is on the left and busy railway yards on the right. We notice the very large railway yards at **Fratton**, after which the train runs between rows of houses into **Portsmouth and Southsea** Station. The magnificent building with the tall clock tower is Portsmouth Guildhall. As we travel slowly on to the **Harbour** Station, looking right, we may just see the masts and rigging of Lord Nelson's flagship "Victory," Portsmouth's most famous monument.

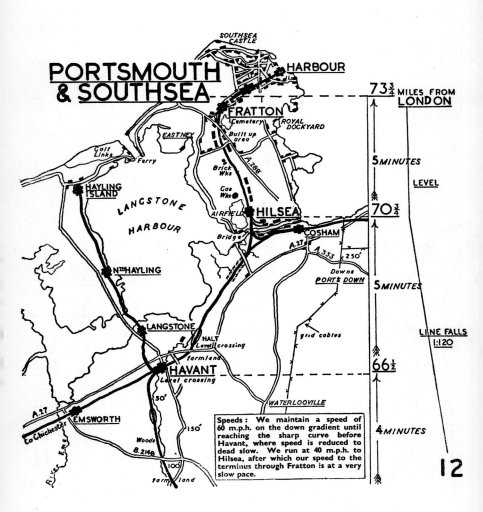

PORTSMOUTH & SOUTHSEA

HARBOUR

SOUTHSEA CASTLE

FRATTON

Cemetery

ROYAL DOCKYARD

Built up area

EASTNEY

Golf Links

Ferry

Brick Wks

A.288

Gas Wks

HAYLING ISLAND

LANGSTONE HARBOUR

AIRFIELD

HILSEA

Bridge

COSHAM

A.27

A.333

250'

Nᵗʰ HAYLING

Downs
PORTS DOWN

LANGSTONE

HALT
Level crossing

farmland

grid cables

HAVANT
Level crossing

WATERLOOVILLE

50'

EMSWORTH

A.27

To Chichester

River Ems

Woods

B.2148

150'

100'

farmland

73¾ MILES FROM LONDON

5 MINUTES

LEVEL

70¾

5 MINUTES

LINE FALLS 1:120

66½

4 MINUTES

Speeds : We maintain a speed of 60 m.p.h. on the down gradient until reaching the sharp curve before Havant, where speed is reduced to dead slow. We run at 40 m.p.h. to Hilsea, after which our speed to the terminus through Fratton is at a very slow pace.

12

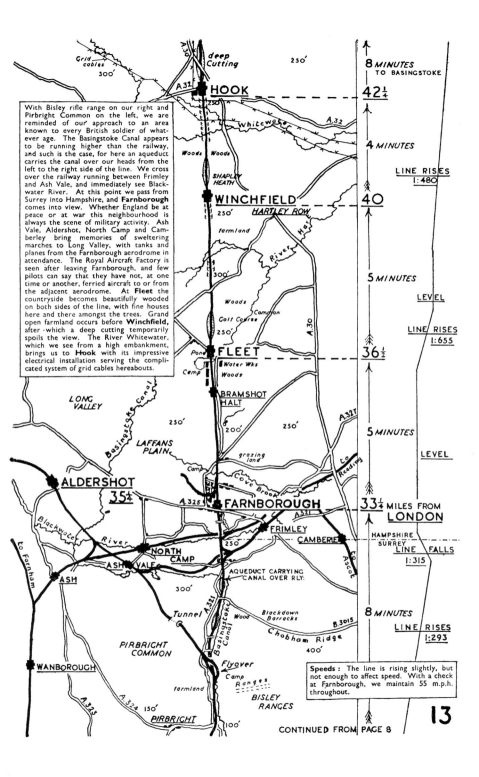

With Bisley rifle range on our right and Pirbright Common on the left, we are reminded of our approach to an area known to every British soldier of whatever age. The Basingstoke Canal appears to be running higher than the railway, and such is the case, for here an aqueduct carries the canal over our heads from the left to the right side of the line. We cross over the railway running between Frimley and Ash Vale, and immediately see Blackwater River. At this point we pass from Surrey into Hampshire, and **Farnborough** comes into view. Whether England be at peace or at war this neighbourhood is always the scene of military activity. Ash Vale, Aldershot, North Camp and Camberley bring memories of sweltering marches to Long Valley, with tanks and planes from the Farnborough aerodrome in attendance. The Royal Aircraft Factory is seen after leaving Farnborough, and few pilots can say that they have not, at one time or another, ferried aircraft to or from the adjacent aerodrome. At **Fleet** the countryside becomes beautifully wooded on both sides of the line, with fine houses here and there amongst the trees. Grand open farmland occurs before **Winchfield**, after which a deep cutting temporarily spoils the view. The River Whitewater, which we see from a high embankment, brings us to **Hook** with its impressive electrical installation serving the complicated system of grid cables hereabouts.

Speeds : The line is rising slightly, but not enough to affect speed. With a check at Farnborough, we maintain 55 m.p.h. throughout.

8 MINUTES TO BASINGSTOKE

42¼

4 MINUTES

LINE RISES 1:480

40

5 MINUTES

LEVEL

LINE RISES 1:655

36½

5 MINUTES

LEVEL

33¼ MILES FROM **LONDON**

HAMPSHIRE
SURREY
LINE FALLS 1:315

8 MINUTES

LINE RISES 1:293

13

CONTINUED FROM PAGE 8

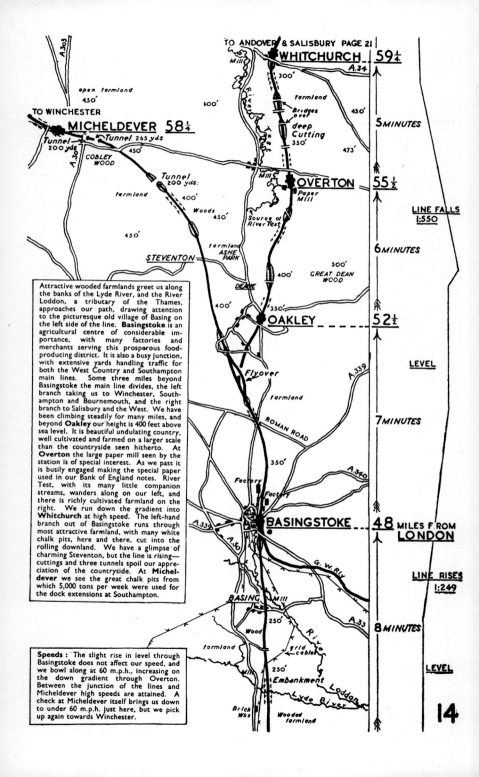

TO ANDOVER & SALISBURY PAGE 21

A.303

open farmland
450'

WHITCHURCH 59¼ A.34

TO WINCHESTER

300'

farmland

Bridges over

450'

Mill

deep Cutting
350'

5 MINUTES

MICHELDEVER 58¼

Tunnel 200 yds
Tunnel 265 yds

COBLEY WOOD
450'

A.30

473'

Tunnel 200 yds
400'

Mill

OVERTON 55½

Paper Mill

farmland

Woods
450'

450'

LINE FALLS 1:550

Source of River Test

6 MINUTES

STEVENTON

farmland ASHE PARK
400'

500'
GREAT DEAN WOOD

DEANE

400'

350'

OAKLEY 52½

LEVEL

Flyover

A.339

farmland

ROMAN ROAD
350'

7 MINUTES

A.340

Factory
Factory

A.339

BASINGSTOKE 48 MILES FROM LONDON

A.30

G.W.Rly.

LINE RISES 1:249

BASING Mill

250'

A.33

8 MINUTES

Wood

grid cables

farmland

250'

Embankment

River Loddon

LEVEL

Mill

Brick Wks

Wooded farmland

Lyde River

14

Attractive wooded farmlands greet us along the banks of the Lyde River, and the River Loddon, a tributary of the Thames, approaches our path, drawing attention to the picturesque old village of Basing on the left side of the line. **Basingstoke** is an agricultural centre of considerable importance, with many factories and merchants serving this prosperous food-producing district. It is also a busy junction, with extensive yards handling traffic for both the West Country and Southampton main lines. Some three miles beyond Basingstoke the main line divides, the left branch taking us to Winchester, Southampton and Bournemouth, and the right branch to Salisbury and the West. We have been climbing steadily for many miles, and beyond **Oakley** our height is 400 feet above sea level. It is beautiful undulating country, well cultivated and farmed on a larger scale than the countryside seen hitherto. At **Overton** the large paper mill seen by the station is of special interest. As we pass it is busily engaged making the special paper used in our Bank of England notes. River Test, with its many little companion streams, wanders along on our left, and there is richly cultivated farmland on the right. We run down the gradient into **Whitchurch** at high speed. The left-hand branch out of Basingstoke runs through most attractive farmland, with many white chalk pits, here and there, cut into the rolling downland. We have a glimpse of charming Steventon, but the line is rising—cuttings and three tunnels spoil our appreciation of the countryside. At **Micheldever** we see the great chalk pits from which 5,000 tons per week were used for the dock extensions at Southampton.

Speeds : The slight rise in level through Basingstoke does not affect our speed, and we bowl along at 60 m.p.h., increasing on the down gradient through Overton. Between the junction of the lines and Micheldever high speeds are attained. A check at Micheldever itself brings us down to under 60 m.p.h. just here, but we pick up again towards Winchester.

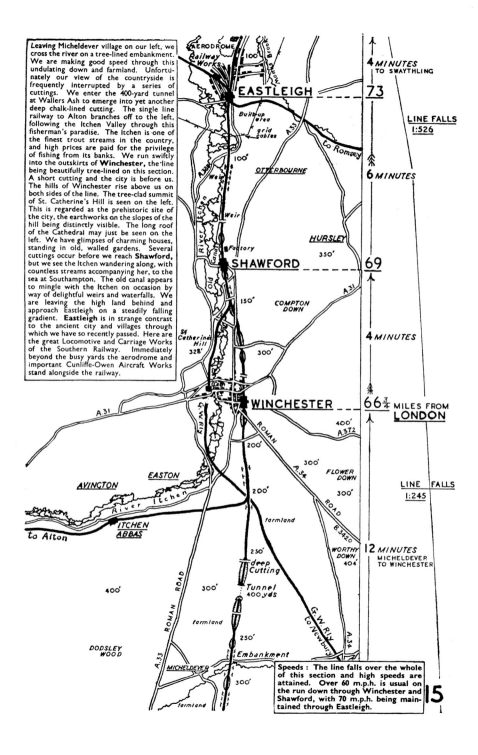

Leaving **Micheldever** village on our left, we cross the river on a tree-lined embankment. We are making good speed through this undulating down and farmland. Unfortunately our view of the countryside is frequently interrupted by a series of cuttings. We enter the 400-yard tunnel at Wallers Ash to emerge into yet another deep chalk-lined cutting. The single line railway to Alton branches off to the left, following the Itchen Valley through this fisherman's paradise. The Itchen is one of the finest trout streams in the country, and high prices are paid for the privilege of fishing from its banks. We run swiftly into the outskirts of **Winchester,** the line being beautifully tree-lined on this section. A short cutting and the city is before us. The hills of Winchester rise above us on both sides of the line. The tree-clad summit of St. Catherine's Hill is seen on the left. This is regarded as the prehistoric site of the city, the earthworks on the slopes of the hill being distinctly visible. The long roof of the Cathedral may just be seen on the left. We have glimpses of charming houses, standing in old, walled gardens. Several cuttings occur before we reach **Shawford,** but we see the Itchen wandering along, with countless streams accompanying her, to the sea at Southampton. The old canal appears to mingle with the Itchen on occasion by way of delightful weirs and waterfalls. We are leaving the high land behind and approach Eastleigh on a steadily falling gradient. **Eastleigh** is in strange contrast to the ancient city and villages through which we have so recently passed. Here are the great Locomotive and Carriage Works of the Southern Railway. Immediately beyond the busy yards the aerodrome and important Cunliffe-Owen Aircraft Works stand alongside the railway.

4 MINUTES TO SWAYTHLING

73

LINE FALLS 1:526

to Romsey

6 MINUTES

69

4 MINUTES

66¾ MILES FROM **LONDON**

LINE FALLS 1:245

12 MINUTES MICHELDEVER TO WINCHESTER

AERODROME
Railway Works
EASTLEIGH
Built-up area
grid cables
A.33
100'
OTTERBOURNE
Weir
River Itchen
Weir
Canal
Factory
HURSLEY
350'
SHAWFORD
A.31
150'
COMPTON DOWN
St. Catherine's Hill 328'
300'
A.31
WINCHESTER
G.W.Rly.
ROMAN
200'
400'
A.372
300'
A.34
FLOWER DOWN
300'
AVINGTON
EASTON
River Itchen
200'
ROAD B.3420
ITCHEN ABBAS
to Alton
farmland
WORTHY DOWN 404'
250'
deep Cutting
400'
300'
Tunnel 400 yds
ROMAN ROAD
farmland
G.W.Rly. to Newbury
A.34
250'
Embankment
DODSLEY WOOD
A.33
MICHELDEVER
300'
farmland

Speeds : The line falls over the whole of this section and high speeds are attained. Over 60 m.p.h. is usual on the run down through Winchester and Shawford, with 70 m.p.h. being maintained through Eastleigh.

15

We approach the built-up area of **Sway-thling**. Shortly after passing the water works on the left, we have our last view of the Itchen, now about to become tidal and flow into the sea at Southampton Water. There is a connection between the next station, **St. Denys**, and Paris. It derives its name from the priory founded there, the convent being subject to the Royal Abbey of St. Denys, near Paris. The great timber yards we see on the left mark the site of Clausentum, the Roman South-ampton. Enormous gas holders at **Northam** dwarf all buildings around, and we are now in a highly industrialised and built-up area. We proceed slowly through the tunnel to **Southampton Central**. The enormous Solent Flour Mill on the left was build on land reclaimed from the estuary of the River Test. Up to a few years ago the river ran quite close to the railway—now it is half a mile away. We see the line of giant cranes lining the docks and almost immediately we travel alongside the wonderful " King George V " Graving Dock. This dock, 1,200 feet long, is the largest in the world, 750,000 tons of concrete being used in its construction. Leaving **Totton**, with its numerous oil tanks and busy factories, we very soon reach open country. By the time we reach **Lyndhurst Road** we are well into the New Forest, where William Rufus met his death. For hundreds of years most of the forest has remained untouched and un-spoiled. From our train it seems there are parts where no foot has ever stepped, the only sign of life amongst the ancient trees and clearings being the wild New Forest ponies, grazing timidly close to the line. We reach **Beaulieu Road**, the same wild forest land stretching for miles around us.

TO BROCKENHURST PAGE 17

LINE FALLS 1:200

6 MINUTES

NEW FOREST

FRAME HEATH

Bridges over

50'

50'

BEAULIEU R? — — 87½

B. 3056

100'

MATLEY HEATH

5 MINUTES

LINE FALLS 1:300

Beaulieu River

50'

forest

forest

LYNDHURST ROAD — — 84¼

A.35

100'

to Fawley

HYTHE

SOUTHAMPTON

Ferry

MARCHWOOD

farmland

A.336

5 MINUTES

LINE RISES 1:200

Ferry

WATER

Cunard Dock

Graving Dock

WOOLSTON

DOCKS

DOCKS'

Mill

TOTTON 82

to Fareham

A.3025

Built-up area

SOUTHAMPTON CENTRAL

50'

River Test

6 MINUTES

78¾ MILES FROM LONDON

NORTHAM

150'

Grid cables

A.3057

to Romsey

4 MINUTES

A.3024

Built-up area

St DENYS

76½

LEVEL

BITTERN

A.27

A.3057

River Itchen

SWAYTHLING

Lock

50'

250'

Speeds : We run into Swaythling at high speed, but slow down approaching St. Denys. Through Northam Junction and Southampton speed is reduced to a minimum, and it is only after leaving Totton that we reach 45 m.p.h. A speed of 60 to 65 m.p.h. is reached on the down gradients through Beaulieu Road.

16

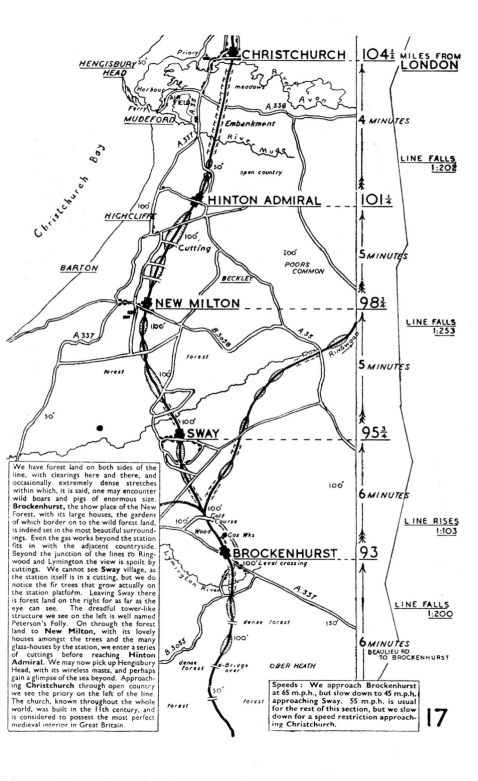

HENGISBURY HEAD

Priory

CHRISTCHURCH 104½ MILES FROM LONDON

meadows

Harbour

AIR FIELD

Ferry

MUDEFORD

Embankment

River Mude

50'

open country

Christchurch Bay

4 MINUTES

LINE FALLS 1:202

HIGHCLIFFE

100'

Cutting

HINTON ADMIRAL 101¼

BARTON

100'

BECKLEY

200'

POORS COMMON

5 MINUTES

A.337

NEW MILTON 98¾

100'

forest

A.35

Ringwood

LINE FALLS 1:253

forest

100'

5 MINUTES

50'

100'

SWAY 95¾

100'

We have forest land on both sides of the line, with clearings here and there, and occasionally extremely dense stretches within which, it is said, one may encounter wild boars and pigs of enormous size. **Brockenhurst**, the show place of the New Forest, with its large houses, the gardens of which border on to the wild forest land, is indeed set in the most beautiful surroundings. Even the gas works beyond the station fits in with the adjacent countryside. Beyond the junction of the lines to Ringwood and Lymington the view is spoilt by cuttings. We cannot see **Sway** village, as the station itself is in a cutting, but we do notice the fir trees that grow actually on the station platform. Leaving Sway there is forest land on the right for as far as the eye can see. The dreadful tower-like structure we see on the left is well named Peterson's Folly. On through the forest land to **New Milton**, with its lovely houses amongst the trees and the many glass-houses by the station, we enter a series of cuttings before reaching **Hinton Admiral**. We may now pick up Hengisbury Head, with its wireless masts, and perhaps gain a glimpse of the sea beyond. Approaching **Christchurch** through open country we see the priory on the left of the line. The church, known throughout the whole world, was built in the 11th century, and is considered to possess the most perfect medieval interior in Great Britain.

100'

6 MINUTES

100'

Golf Course

Wood

Gas Wks

LINE RISES 1:103

BROCKENHURST 93

100' Level crossing

Lymington River

A.337

LINE FALLS 1:200

dense forest

150'

B.3055

100'

6 MINUTES

BEAULIEU RD TO BROCKENHURST

dense forest

a-Bridge over

OBER HEATH

50'

forest

forest

Speeds : We approach Brockenhurst at 65 m.p.h., but slow down to 45 m.p.h. approaching Sway. 55 m.p.h. is usual for the rest of this section, but we slow down for a speed restriction approaching Christchurch.

17

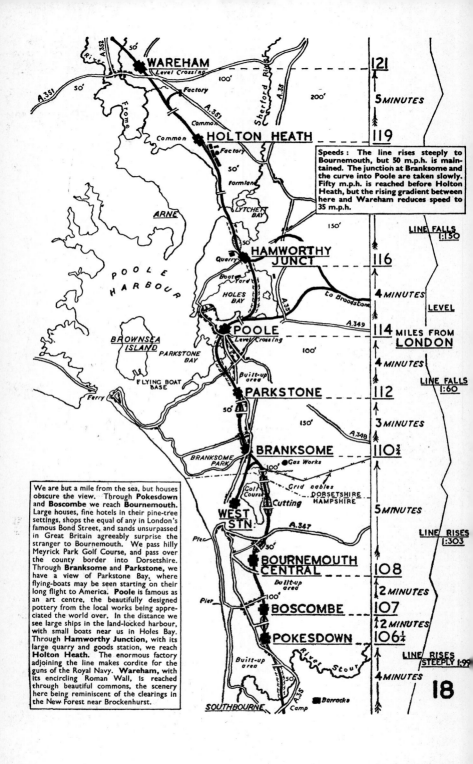

WAREHAM
Level Crossing

River A.352

50'

A.351

50'

River Frome

100'

Factory

A.351

Common

Sherford River

A.35

200'

Common

HOLTON HEATH

Factory

50'

Farmland

LYTCHETT BAY

ARNE

P O O L E
H A R B O U R

Quarry

HAMWORTHY
JUNCT

Boat Yard

HOLES BAY

to Broadstone

150'

A.35

BROWNSEA
ISLAND

PARKSTONE
BAY

FLYING BOAT
BASE

A.349

POOLE
Level Crossing

100'

Ferry

Built-up area

PARKSTONE

50'

150'

A.348

BRANKSOME
PARK

BRANKSOME

Gas Works

100'

Golf Course

Grid cables

DORSETSHIRE
HAMPSHIRE

Cutting

WEST
STN.

A.347

Pier

50'

BOURNEMOUTH
CENTRAL

Built-up area

100'

Pier

BOSCOMBE

POKESDOWN

Built-up area

50'

River Stour

Barracks

SOUTHBOURNE

Camp

A.35

121

5 MINUTES

119

Speeds : The line rises steeply to Bournemouth, but 50 m.p.h. is maintained. The junction at Branksome and the curve into Poole are taken slowly. Fifty m.p.h. is reached before Holton Heath, but the rising gradient between here and Wareham reduces speed to 35 m.p.h.

150'

LINE FALLS
1:150

116

4 MINUTES

LEVEL

114   MILES FROM
LONDON

4 MINUTES

LINE FALLS
1:60

112

3 MINUTES

110¾

5 MINUTES

LINE RISES
1:303

108

2 MINUTES

107

2 MINUTES

106½

LINE RISES
STEEPLY 1:99

4 MINUTES

18

We are but a mile from the sea, but houses obscure the view. Through **Pokesdown** and **Boscombe** we reach **Bournemouth.** Large houses, fine hotels in their pine-tree settings, shops the equal of any in London's famous Bond Street, and sands unsurpassed in Great Britain agreeably surprise the stranger to Bournemouth. We pass hilly Meyrick Park Golf Course, and pass over the county border into Dorsetshire. Through **Branksome** and **Parkstone,** we have a view of Parkstone Bay, where flying-boats may be seen starting on their long flight to America. **Poole** is famous as an art centre, the beautifully designed pottery from the local works being appreciated the world over. In the distance we see large ships in the land-locked harbour, with small boats near us in Holes Bay. Through **Hamworthy Junction,** with its large quarry and goods station, we reach **Holton Heath.** The enormous factory adjoining the line makes cordite for the guns of the Royal Navy. **Wareham,** with its encircling Roman Wall, is reached through beautiful commons, the scenery here being reminiscent of the clearings in the New Forest near Brockenhurst.

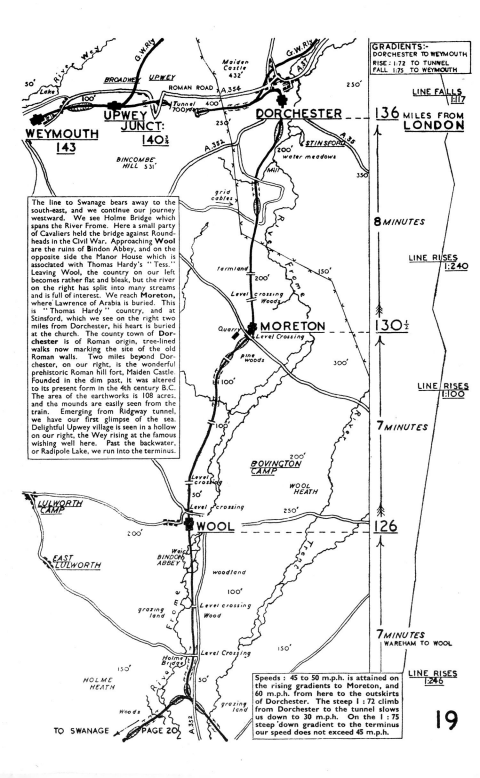

GRADIENTS:-
DORCHESTER TO WEYMOUTH
RISE : 1:72 TO TUNNEL
FALL 1:75 TO WEYMOUTH

LINE FALLS 1:117

136 MILES FROM **LONDON**

WEYMOUTH **143**

UPWEY JUNCT: **140¼**

50' Lake
100'
River Wey
G.W.R^y.
BROADWEY
UPWEY
ROMAN ROAD A.354
Tunnel 700yds
400'
Maiden Castle 432'
G.W.R^y.
A.37
250'

DORCHESTER

BINCOMBE HILL 531'
A.352
250'
200' STINSFORD
water meadows
A.35
Mill
350'

grid cables

8 MINUTES

LINE RISES 1:240

The line to Swanage bears away to the south-east, and we continue our journey westward. We see Holme Bridge which spans the River Frome. Here a small party of Cavaliers held the bridge against Roundheads in the Civil War. Approaching **Wool** are the ruins of **B**indon Abbey, and on the opposite side the Manor House which is associated with Thomas Hardy's "Tess." Leaving Wool, the country on our left becomes rather flat and bleak, but the river on the right has split into many streams and is full of interest. We reach **Moreton**, where Lawrence of Arabia is buried. This is "Thomas Hardy" country, and at Stinsford, which we see on the right two miles from Dorchester, his heart is buried at the church. The county town of **Dorchester** is of Roman origin, tree-lined walks now marking the site of the old Roman walls. Two miles beyond Dorchester, on our right, is the wonderful prehistoric Roman hill fort, Maiden Castle. Founded in the dim past, it was altered to its present form in the 4th century B.C. The area of the earthworks is 108 acres, and the mounds are easily seen from the train. Emerging from Ridgway tunnel, we have our first glimpse of the sea. Delightful Upwey village is seen in a hollow on our right, the Wey rising at the famous wishing well here. Past the backwater, or Radipole Lake, we run into the terminus.

farmland 200'
150'
Level crossing Woods

Quarry
MORETON
Level Crossing
130½

pine woods
300'
100'

100'

7 MINUTES

LINE RISES 1:100

100'

200'
BOVINGTON CAMP
WOOL HEATH

LULWORTH CAMP
Level crossing
50'
Level crossing
250'

EAST LULWORTH
200'

WOOL **126**

Weir BINDON ABBEY
woodland
100'
grazing land
Level crossing Wood
River Trent
150'

7 MINUTES
WAREHAM TO WOOL

LINE RISES 1:246

Holme Bridge
50'
HOLME HEATH
150'
Woods
grazing land
River Frome
Level Crossing

TO SWANAGE   PAGE 20
A.352

Speeds : 45 to 50 m.p.h. is attained on the rising gradients to Moreton, and 60 m.p.h. from here to the outskirts of Dorchester. The steep 1 : 72 climb from Dorchester to the tunnel slows us down to 30 m.p.h. On the 1 : 75 steep down gradient to the terminus our speed does not exceed 45 m.p.h.

19

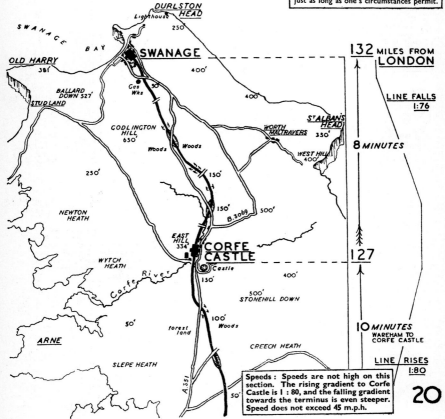

This is lovely moorland country with woods bordering the line. High ground towers above us on the right, whilst on the left we look across the moorland to Arne and Poole Bay. **Corfe Castle** lies in a gap in the Purbeck Hills. The ruins of the castle stand on a hillock just before the station, completely dominating the quaint and picturesque grey stone village grouped beneath. The origin of the castle is obscure, but, according to tradition, it was the scene of the murder of King Edward in A.D. 978. A busy creamery stands in the station yard, with a hill rising 200 feet sheer behind it. Woods alongside the line intermingle with stretches of gorse-covered common. We are nearly at the seaside. Hills shelter **Swanage** from all but the soft winds from the south, and bathing between Peveril Point and Ballard Point is a delight for those who demand that their swimming and beach idling shall not be spoilt by unkind winds. The population of Swanage is given as 6,000. By the presence of the several fine hotels, and the number of modern shops ready to greet the visitor, it is apparent that a large number of holiday-makers must swell the population both in and out of the season. The reason is not far to seek. A few hours spent in Swanage determines one to come again ; to come again soon, and next time to stay just as long as one's circumstances permit.

ENGLISH CHANNEL

DURLSTON HEAD
Lighthouse 250'

SWANAGE
SWANAGE BAY

OLD HARRY 381

BALLARD DOWN 527'
STUDLAND

Gas Wks 50'

GODLINGTON HILL 650'

400'

400'

St. ALBAN'S HEAD 350'

WORTH MALTRAVERS

WEST HILL 400'

Woods   Woods

250'

150'

150'

B.3069   500'

NEWTON HEATH

EAST HILL 334

CORFE CASTLE
Castle

150'

WYTCH HEATH

Corfe River

400'

500' STONEHILL DOWN

ARNE

50'

forest land

100' Woods

CREECH HEATH

SLEPE HEATH

A.351

50'

132 MILES FROM LONDON

LINE FALLS 1:76

8 MINUTES

127

10 MINUTES
WAREHAM TO CORFE CASTLE

LINE RISES 1:80

Speeds : Speeds are not high on this section. The rising gradient to Corfe Castle is 1 : 80, and the falling gradient towards the terminus is even steeper. Speed does not exceed 45 m.p.h.

20

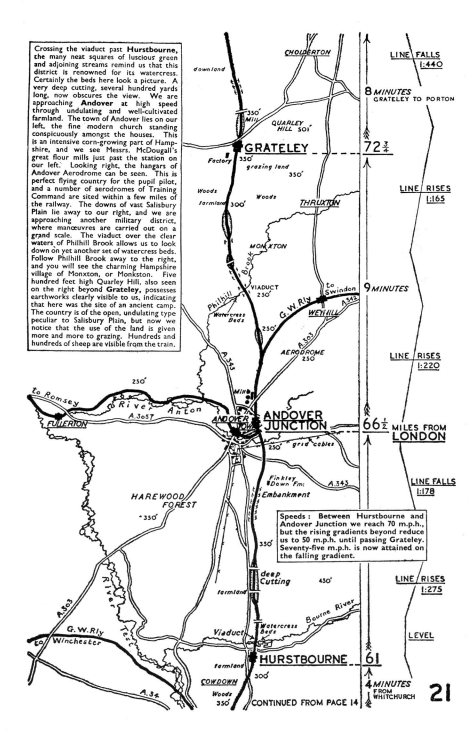

Crossing the viaduct past **Hurstbourne**, the many neat squares of luscious green and adjoining streams remind us that this district is renowned for its watercress. Certainly the beds here look a picture. A very deep cutting, several hundred yards long, now obscures the view. We are approaching **Andover** at high speed through undulating and well-cultivated farmland. The town of Andover lies on our left, the fine modern church standing conspicuously amongst the houses. This is an intensive corn-growing part of Hampshire, and we see Messrs. McDougall's great flour mills just past the station on our left. Looking right, the hangars of Andover Aerodrome can be seen. This is perfect flying country for the pupil pilot, and a number of aerodromes of Training Command are sited within a few miles of the railway. The downs of vast Salisbury Plain lie away to our right, and we are approaching another military district, where manœuvres are carried out on a grand scale. The viaduct over the clear waters of Philhill Brook allows us to look down on yet another set of watercress beds. Follow Philhill Brook away to the right, and you will see the charming Hampshire village of Monxton, or Monkston. Five hundred feet high Quarley Hill, also seen on the right beyond **Grateley**, possesses earthworks clearly visible to us, indicating that here was the site of an ancient camp. The country is of the open, undulating type peculiar to Salisbury Plain, but now we notice that the use of the land is given more and more to grazing. Hundreds and hundreds of sheep are visible from the train.

Speeds: Between Hurstbourne and Andover Junction we reach 70 m.p.h., but the rising gradients beyond reduce us to 50 m.p.h. until passing Grateley. Seventy-five m.p.h. is now attained on the falling gradient.

CHOLDERTON

downland

350' Mill

QUARLEY HILL 501'

GRATELEY

Factory 350'

grazing land 350'

Woods

farmland 300'   Woods

THRUXTON

MONXTON

Philhill Brook

VIADUCT 250'

to Swindon

G.W.Rly   WEYHILL   A.342

Watercress Beds

250'

A.303

AERODROME 250

250'

to Romsey   River Anton   A.3057

FULLERTON

Mill

ANDOVER JUNCTION

250'   grid cables

HAREWOOD FOREST

+350'

Finkley Down Fm: A.343

Embankment

River Test

350'

A.303

G.W.Rly to Winchester

deep Cutting   450'

farmland

Viaduct   Watercress Beds   Bourne River

farmland

HURSTBOURNE

COWDOWN   300'

Woods   350'   CONTINUED FROM PAGE 14

LINE FALLS 1:440

8 MINUTES GRATELEY TO PORTON

72¾

LINE RISES 1:165

9 MINUTES

LINE RISES 1:220

66½ MILES FROM LONDON

LINE FALLS 1:178

LINE RISES 1:275

LEVEL

61

4 MINUTES FROM WHITCHURCH

21

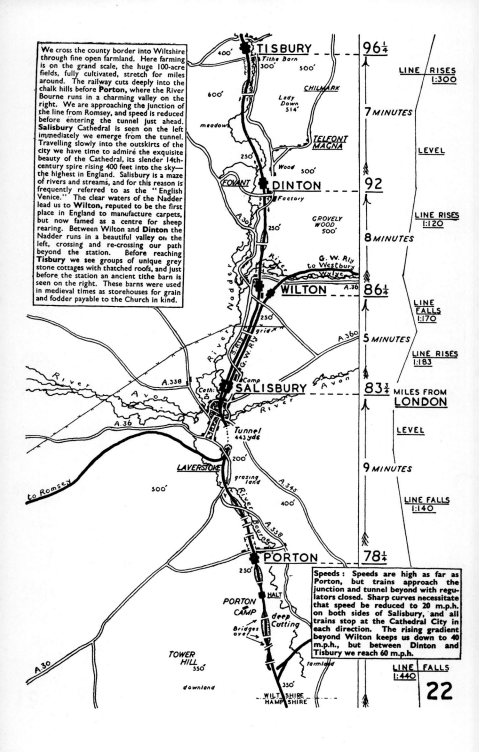

We cross the county border into Wiltshire through fine open farmland. Here farming is on the grand scale, the huge 100-acre fields, fully cultivated, stretch for miles around. The railway cuts deeply into the chalk hills before **Porton**, where the River Bourne runs in a charming valley on the right. We are approaching the junction of the line from Romsey, and speed is reduced before entering the tunnel just ahead. **Salisbury** Cathedral is seen on the left immediately we emerge from the tunnel. Travelling slowly into the outskirts of the city we have time to admire the exquisite beauty of the Cathedral, its slender 14th-century spire rising 400 feet into the sky—the highest in England. Salisbury is a maze of rivers and streams, and for this reason is frequently referred to as the "English Venice." The clear waters of the Nadder lead us to **Wilton**, reputed to be the first place in England to manufacture carpets, but now famed as a centre for sheep rearing. Between Wilton and **Dinton** the Nadder runs in a beautiful valley on the left, crossing and re-crossing our path beyond the station. Before reaching **Tisbury** we see groups of unique grey stone cottages with thatched roofs, and just before the station an ancient tithe barn is seen on the right. These barns were used in medieval times as storehouses for grain and fodder payable to the Church in kind.

TISBURY — 96¼

LINE RISES 1:300

7 MINUTES

LEVEL

DINTON — 92

LINE RISES 1:120

8 MINUTES

WILTON — 86¼

LINE FALLS 1:170

5 MINUTES

LINE RISES 1:183

SALISBURY — 83¾ MILES FROM LONDON

LEVEL

9 MINUTES

LINE FALLS 1:140

PORTON — 78¼

Speeds: Speeds are high as far as Porton, but trains approach the junction and tunnel beyond with regulators closed. Sharp curves necessitate that speed be reduced to 20 m.p.h. on both sides of Salisbury, and all trains stop at the Cathedral City in each direction. The rising gradient beyond Wilton keeps us down to 40 m.p.h., but between Dinton and Tisbury we reach 60 m.p.h.

LINE FALLS 1:440

22

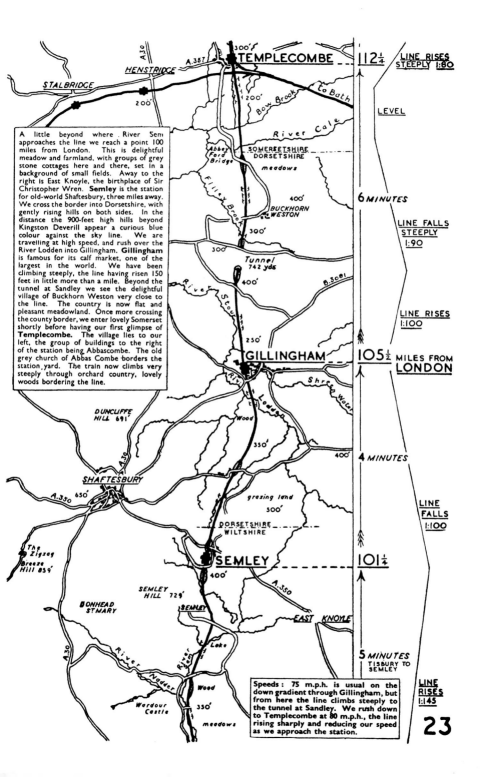

A little beyond where River Sem approaches the line we reach a point 100 miles from London. This is delightful meadow and farmland, with groups of grey stone cottages here and there, set in a background of small fields. Away to the right is East Knoyle, the birthplace of Sir Christopher Wren. **Semley** is the station for old-world Shaftesbury, three miles away. We cross the border into Dorsetshire, with gently rising hills on both sides. In the distance the 900-feet high hills beyond Kingston Deverill appear a curious blue colour against the sky line. We are travelling at high speed, and rush over the River Lodden into Gillingham. **Gillingham** is famous for its calf market, one of the largest in the world. We have been climbing steeply, the line having risen 150 feet in little more than a mile. Beyond the tunnel at Sandley we see the delightful village of Buckhorn Weston very close to the line. The country is now flat and pleasant meadowland. Once more crossing the county border, we enter lovely Somerset shortly before having our first glimpse of **Templecombe.** The village lies to our left, the group of buildings to the right of the station being Abbascombe. The old grey church of Abbas Combe borders the station yard. The train now climbs steeply through orchard country, lovely woods bordering the line.

Speeds : 75 m.p.h. is usual on the down gradient through Gillingham, but from here the line climbs steeply to the tunnel at Sandley. We rush down to Templecombe at 80 m.p.h., the line rising sharply and reducing our speed as we approach the station.

TEMPLECOMBE — 112¼ LINE RISES STEEPLY 1:80

LEVEL

6 MINUTES

LINE FALLS STEEPLY 1:90

LINE RISES 1:100

GILLINGHAM — 105½ MILES FROM LONDON

4 MINUTES

LINE FALLS 1:100

SEMLEY — 101¼

5 MINUTES TISBURY TO SEMLEY

LINE RISES 1:145

23

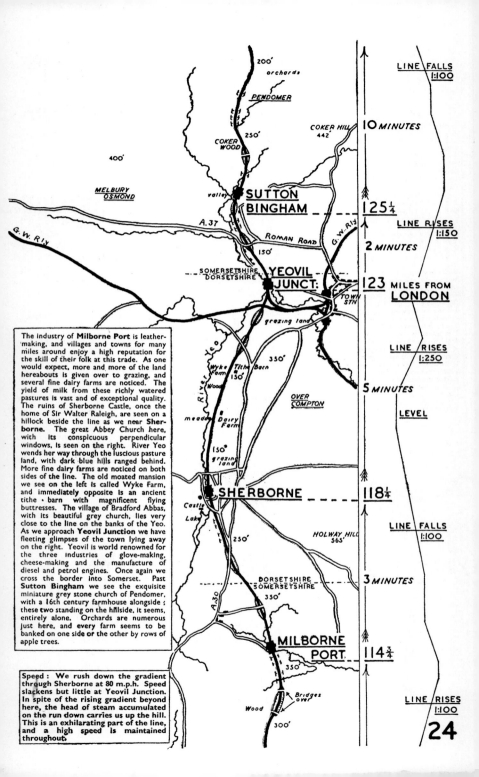

The industry of **Milborne Port** is leather-making, and villages and towns for many miles around enjoy a high reputation for the skill of their folk at this trade. As one would expect, more and more of the land hereabouts is given over to grazing, and several fine dairy farms are noticed. The yield of milk from these richly watered pastures is vast and of exceptional quality. The ruins of Sherborne Castle, once the home of Sir Walter Raleigh, are seen on a hillock beside the line as we near **Sherborne**. The great Abbey Church here, with its conspicuous perpendicular windows, is seen on the right. River Yeo wends her way through the luscious pasture land, with dark blue hills ranged behind. More fine dairy farms are noticed on both sides of the line. The old moated mansion we see on the left is called Wyke Farm, and immediately opposite is an ancient tithe · barn with magnificent flying buttresses. The village of Bradford Abbas, with its beautiful grey church, lies very close to the line on the banks of the Yeo. As we approach **Yeovil Junction** we have fleeting glimpses of the town lying away on the right. Yeovil is world renowned for the three industries of glove-making, cheese-making and the manufacture of diesel and petrol engines. Once again we cross the border into Somerset. Past **Sutton Bingham** we see the exquisite miniature grey stone church of Pendomer, with a 16th century farmhouse alongside ; these two standing on the hillside, it seems, entirely alone. Orchards are numerous just here, and every farm seems to be banked on one side or the other by rows of apple trees.

Speed : We rush down the gradient through Sherborne at 80 m.p.h. Speed slackens but little at Yeovil Junction. In spite of the rising gradient beyond here, the head of steam accumulated on the run down carries us up the hill. This is an exhilarating part of the line, and a high speed is maintained throughout.

LINE FALLS 1:100

10 MINUTES

$125\frac{1}{4}$

LINE RISES 1:150

2 MINUTES

123 MILES FROM LONDON

LINE RISES 1:250

5 MINUTES

LEVEL

$118\frac{1}{4}$

LINE FALLS 1:100

3 MINUTES

$114\frac{3}{4}$

LINE RISES 1:100

24

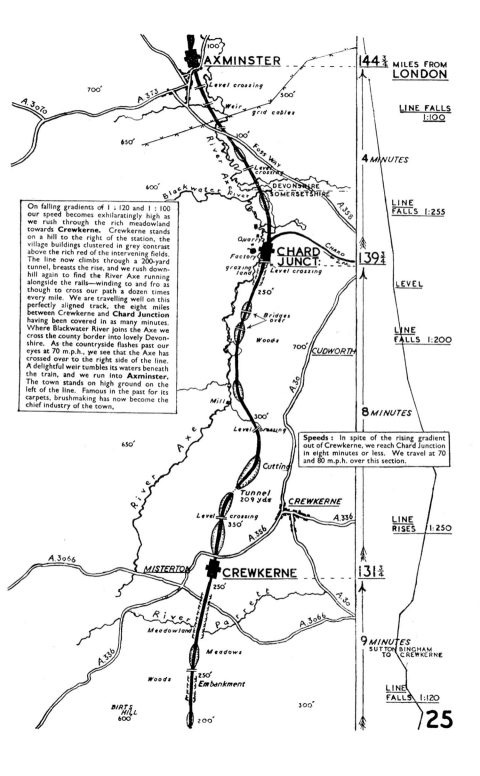

On falling gradients of 1 : 120 and 1 : 100 our speed becomes exhilaratingly high as we rush through the rich meadowland towards **Crewkerne.** Crewkerne stands on a hill to the right of the station, the village buildings clustered in grey contrast above the rich red of the intervening fields. The line now climbs through a 200-yard tunnel, breasts the rise, and we rush down-hill again to find the River Axe running alongside the rails—winding to and fro as though to cross our path a dozen times every mile. We are travelling well on this perfectly aligned track, the eight miles between Crewkerne and **Chard Junction** having been covered in as many minutes. Where Blackwater River joins the Axe we cross the county border into lovely Devonshire. As the countryside flashes past our eyes at 70 m.p.h., we see that the Axe has crossed over to the right side of the line. A delightful weir tumbles its waters beneath the train, and we run into **Axminster.** The town stands on high ground on the left of the line. Famous in the past for its carpets, brushmaking has now become the chief industry of the town.

Speeds: In spite of the rising gradient out of Crewkerne, we reach Chard Junction in eight minutes or less. We travel at 70 and 80 m.p.h. over this section.

AXMINSTER

144¾ MILES FROM LONDON

LINE FALLS 1:100

4 MINUTES

LINE FALLS 1:255

CHARD JUNCT:

139¾

LEVEL

LINE FALLS 1:200

CUDWORTH

8 MINUTES

CREWKERNE

LINE RISES 1:250

131¾

9 MINUTES SUTTON BINGHAM TO CREWKERNE

LINE FALLS 1:120

MISTERTON

Tunnel 209 yds

Cutting

Mill

Embankment

Meadowlands

Meadows

Woods

BIRTS HILL 600

25

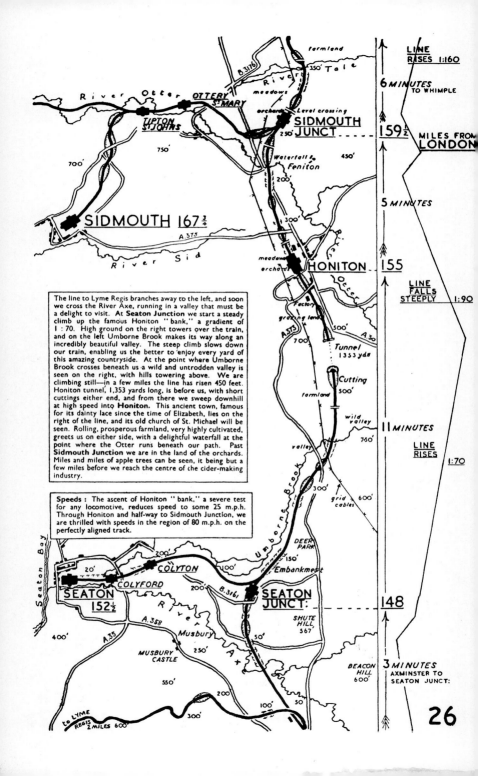

The line to Lyme Regis branches away to the left, and soon we cross the River Axe, running in a valley that must be a delight to visit. At **Seaton Junction** we start a steady climb up the famous Honiton "bank," a gradient of 1 : 70. High ground on the right towers over the train, and on the left Umborne Brook makes its way along an incredibly beautiful valley. The steep climb slows down our train, enabling us the better to enjoy every yard of this amazing countryside. At the point where Umborne Brook crosses beneath us a wild and untrodden valley is seen on the right, with hills towering above. We are climbing still—in a few miles the line has risen 450 feet. Honiton tunnel, 1,353 yards long, is before us, with short cuttings either end, and from there we sweep downhill at high speed into **Honiton**. This ancient town, famous for its dainty lace since the time of Elizabeth, lies on the right of the line, and its old church of St. Michael will be seen. Rolling, prosperous farmland, very highly cultivated, greets us on either side, with a delightful waterfall at the point where the Otter runs beneath our path. Past **Sidmouth Junction** we are in the land of the orchards. Miles and miles of apple trees can be seen, it being but a few miles before we reach the centre of the cider-making industry.

Speeds : The ascent of Honiton "bank," a severe test for any locomotive, reduces speed to some 25 m.p.h. Through Honiton and half-way to Sidmouth Junction, we are thrilled with speeds in the region of 80 m.p.h. on the perfectly aligned track.

26

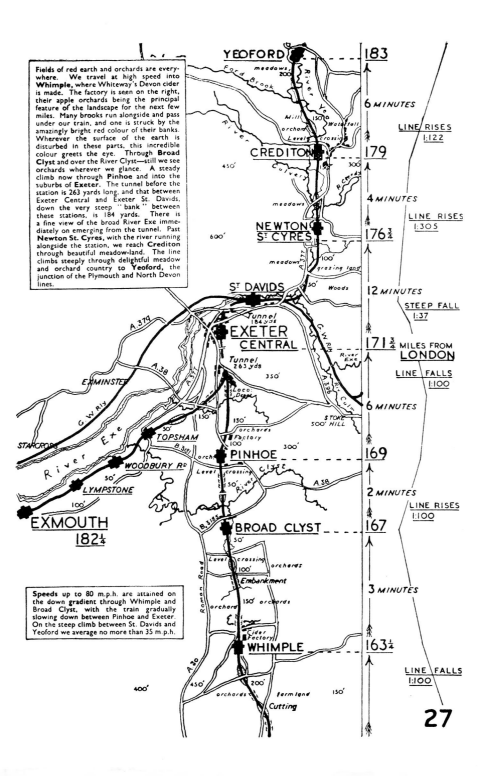

Fields of red earth and orchards are every-where. We travel at high speed into **Whimple**, where Whiteway's Devon cider is made. The factory is seen on the right, their apple orchards being the principal feature of the landscape for the next few miles. Many brooks run alongside and pass under our train, and one is struck by the amazingly bright red colour of their banks. Wherever the surface of the earth is disturbed in these parts, this incredible colour greets the eye. Through **Broad Clyst** and over the River Clyst—still we see orchards wherever we glance. A steady climb now through **Pinhoe** and into the suburbs of **Exeter**. The tunnel before the station is 263 yards long, and that between Exeter Central and Exeter St. Davids, down the very steep "bank" between these stations, is 184 yards. There is a fine view of the broad River Exe immediately on emerging from the tunnel. Past **Newton St. Cyres**, with the river running alongside the station, we reach **Crediton** through beautiful meadow-land. The line climbs steeply through delightful meadow and orchard country to **Yeoford**, the junction of the Plymouth and North Devon lines.

Speeds up to 80 m.p.h. are attained on the down **gradient** through Whimple and Broad Clyst, with the train gradually slowing down between Pinhoe and Exeter. On the steep climb between St. Davids and Yeoford we average no more than 35 m.p.h.

YEOFORD

183

6 MINUTES

LINE RISES
1:122

CREDITON

179

4 MINUTES

LINE RISES
1:305

NEWTON
ST CYRES

176¾

12 MINUTES

STEEP FALL
1:37

ST DAVIDS

EXETER
CENTRAL

171¾ MILES FROM
LONDON

LINE FALLS
1:100

6 MINUTES

PINHOE

169

2 MINUTES

LINE RISES
1:100

EXMOUTH
182¼

BROAD CLYST

167

3 MINUTES

WHIMPLE

163¼

LINE FALLS
1:100

27

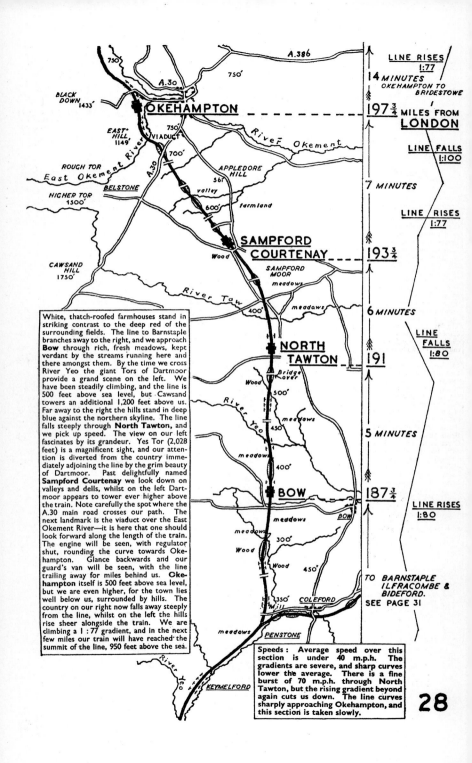

LINE RISES 1:77

14 MINUTES
OKEHAMPTON TO BRIDESTOWE

197¾ MILES FROM LONDON

LINE FALLS 1:100

7 MINUTES

LINE RISES 1:77

193¾

6 MINUTES

LINE FALLS 1:80

191

5 MINUTES

187¾

LINE RISES 1:80

TO BARNSTAPLE ILFRACOMBE & BIDEFORD.
SEE PAGE 31

White, thatch-roofed farmhouses stand in striking contrast to the deep red of the surrounding fields. The line to Barnstaple branches away to the right, and we approach **Bow** through rich, fresh meadows, kept verdant by the streams running here and there amongst them. By the time we cross River Yeo the giant Tors of Dartmoor provide a grand scene on the left. We have been steadily climbing, and the line is 500 feet above sea level, but Cawsand towers an additional 1,200 feet above us. Far away to the right the hills stand in deep blue against the northern skyline. The line falls steeply through **North Tawton**, and we pick up speed. The view on our left fascinates by its grandeur. Yes Tor (2,028 feet) is a magnificent sight, and our attention is diverted from the country immediately adjoining the line by the grim beauty of Dartmoor. Past delightfully named **Sampford Courtenay** we look down on valleys and dells, whilst on the left Dartmoor appears to tower ever higher above the train. Note carefully the spot where the A.30 main road crosses our path. The next landmark is the viaduct over the East Okement River—it is here that one should look forward along the length of the train. The engine will be seen, with regulator shut, rounding the curve towards Okehampton. Glance backwards and our guard's van will be seen, with the line trailing away for miles behind us. **Okehampton** itself is 500 feet above sea level, but we are even higher, for the town lies well below us, surrounded by hills. The country on our right now falls away steeply from the line, whilst on the left the hills rise sheer alongside the train. We are climbing a 1 : 77 gradient, and in the next few miles our train will have reached the summit of the line, 950 feet above the sea.

Speeds : Average speed over this section is under 40 m.p.h. The gradients are severe, and sharp curves lower the average. There is a fine burst of 70 m.p.h. through North Tawton, but the rising gradient beyond again cuts us down. The line curves sharply approaching Okehampton, and this section is taken slowly.

28

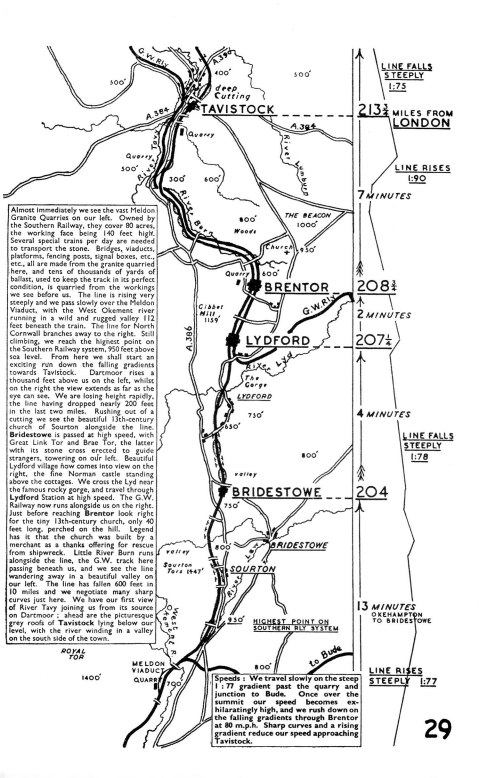

Map labels:

G.W. RLY
A.390
400'
500'
deep Cutting
TAVISTOCK
A.384
500'
River Lumburn
A.384
Quarry
Quarry
500'
River Tavy
300'
600'
River Burn
800'
Woods
THE BEACON
1000'
Church 950'
Quarry 600'
BRENTOR
Gibbet Hill 1159'
G.W. Rly
A.386
LYDFORD
River Lyd
The Gorge
LYDFORD
750'
650'
800'
valley
BRIDESTOWE
750'
BRIDESTOWE
valley
800'
Sourton Tors 1447'
SOURTON
River Lew
950'
West Okement R.
ROYAL TOR
1400'
MELDON VIADUCT
QUARRY
790'
800'
to Bude
HIGHEST POINT ON SOUTHERN RLY SYSTEM

Right-hand scale:

LINE FALLS STEEPLY 1:75
213¾ MILES FROM LONDON
LINE RISES 1:90
7 MINUTES
208¾
2 MINUTES
207¼
4 MINUTES
LINE FALLS STEEPLY 1:78
204
13 MINUTES OKEHAMPTON TO BRIDESTOWE
LINE RISES STEEPLY 1:77

Left text box:

Almost immediately we see the vast Meldon Granite Quarries on our left. Owned by the Southern Railway, they cover 80 acres, the working face being 140 feet high. Several special trains per day are needed to transport the stone. Bridges, viaducts, platforms, fencing posts, signal boxes, etc., etc., all are made from the granite quarried here, and tens of thousands of yards of ballast, used to keep the track in its perfect condition, is quarried from the workings we see before us. The line is rising very steeply and we pass slowly over the Meldon Viaduct, with the West Okement river running in a wild and rugged valley 112 feet beneath the train. The line for North Cornwall branches away to the right. Still climbing, we reach the highest point on the Southern Railway system, 950 feet above sea level. From here we shall start an exciting run down the falling gradients towards Tavistock. Dartmoor rises a thousand feet above us on the left, whilst on the right the view extends as far as the eye can see. We are losing height rapidly, the line having dropped nearly 200 feet in the last two miles. Rushing out of a cutting we see the beautiful 13th-century church of Sourton alongside the line. **Bridestowe** is passed at high speed, with Great Link Tor and Brae Tor, the latter with its stone cross erected to guide strangers, towering on our left. Beautiful Lydford village how comes into view on the right, the fine Norman castle standing above the cottages. We cross the Lyd near the famous rocky gorge, and travel through Lydford Station at high speed. The G.W. Railway now runs alongside us on the right. Just before reaching **Brentor** look right for the tiny 13th-century church, only 40 feet long, perched on the hill. Legend has it that the church was built by a merchant as a thanks offering for rescue from shipwreck. Little River Burn runs alongside the line, the G.W. track here passing beneath us, and we see the line wandering away in a beautiful valley on our left. The line has fallen 600 feet in 10 miles and we negotiate many sharp curves just here. We have our first view of River Tavy joining us from its source on Dartmoor ; ahead are the picturesque grey roofs of **Tavistock** lying below our level, with the river winding in a valley on the south side of the town.

Bottom text box:

Speeds : We travel slowly on the steep 1 : 77 gradient past the quarry and junction to Bude. Once over the summit our speed becomes exhilaratingly high, and we rush down on the falling gradients through Brentor at 80 m.p.h. Sharp curves and a rising gradient reduce our speed approaching Tavistock.

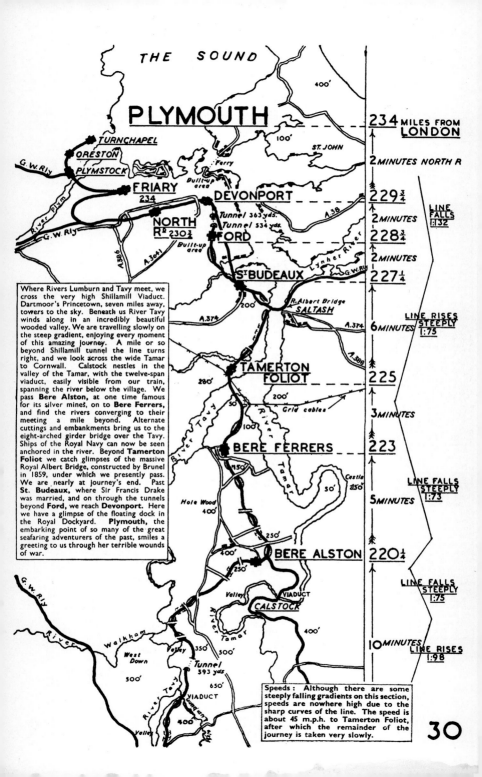

THE SOUND

PLYMOUTH

TURNCHAPEL
ORESTON
PLYMSTOCK
G.W.Rly
St. John
Ferry
100'
Built-up area
FRIARY
234
DEVONPORT
A.38
Tunnel 363 yds.
NORTH
RD 230½
Tunnel 534 yds.
FORD
Built-up area
Lynher River
A.3cri
A.386
A.374
River Plym
G.W. Rly
St BUDEAUX
200'
R. Albert Bridge
SALTASH
G.W.Rly
A.374
A.386
TAMERTON
FOLIOT
280'
200'
50
100'
Grid cables
River Tamar
BERE FERRERS
150'
Castle 250'
50'
Hole Wood 400'
250'
400'
250'
BERE ALSTON
Valley
VIADUCT
CALSTOCK
400'
River Tamar
River Walkham
West Down
500'
Valley
350'
500'
Tunnel 393 yds
650'
VIADUCT
River Tavy
400'
Valley

234 MILES FROM LONDON
↑ 2 MINUTES NORTH R
229¾
↑ 2 MINUTES
228¾
↑ 2 MINUTES
227¼
↑ 6 MINUTES
225
↑ 3 MINUTES
223
↑ 5 MINUTES
220¼
↑ 10 MINUTES

LINE FALLS 1:32
LINE RISES STEEPLY 1:75
LINE FALLS STEEPLY 1:73
LINE FALLS STEEPLY 1:75
LINE RISES 1:98

Where Rivers Lumburn and Tavy meet, we cross the very high Shillamill Viaduct. Dartmoor's Princetown, seven miles away, towers to the sky. Beneath us River Tavy winds along in an incredibly beautiful wooded valley. We are travelling slowly on the steep gradient, enjoying every moment of this amazing journey. A mile or so beyond Shillamill tunnel the line turns right, and we look across the wide Tamar to Cornwall. Calstock nestles in the valley of the Tamar, with the twelve-span viaduct, easily visible from our train, spanning the river below the village. We pass **Bere Alston**, at one time famous for its silver mines, on to **Bere Ferrers**, and find the rivers converging to their meeting a mile beyond. Alternate cuttings and embankments bring us to the eight-arched girder bridge over the Tavy. Ships of the Royal Navy can now be seen anchored in the river. Beyond **Tamerton Foliot** we catch glimpses of the massive Royal Albert Bridge, constructed by Brunel in 1859, under which we presently pass. We are nearly at journey's end. Past **St. Budeaux**, where Sir Francis Drake was married, and on through the tunnels beyond **Ford**, we reach **Devonport**. Here we have a glimpse of the floating dock in the Royal Dockyard. **Plymouth**, the embarking point of so many of the great seafaring adventurers of the past, smiles a greeting to us through her terrible wounds of war.

Speeds: Although there are some steeply falling gradients on this section, speeds are nowhere high due to the sharp curves of the line. The speed is about 45 m.p.h. to Tamerton Foliot, after which the remainder of the journey is taken very slowly.

30

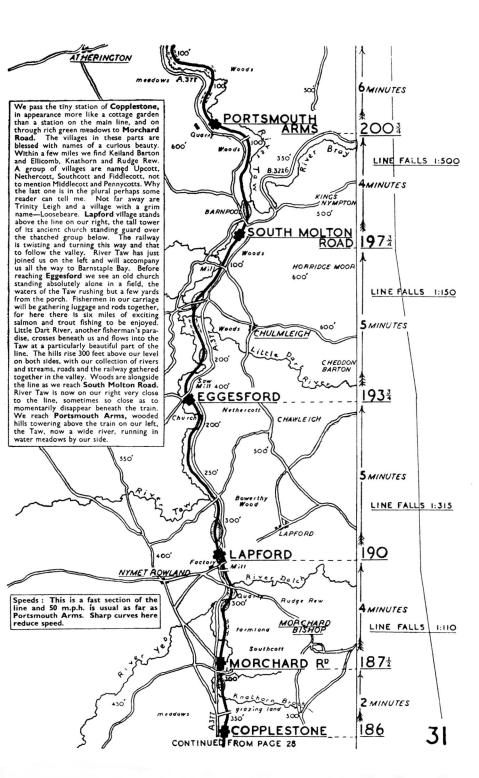

We pass the tiny station of **Copplestone**, in appearance more like a cottage garden than a station on the main line, and on through rich green meadows near **Morchard Road**. The villages in these parts are blessed with names of a curious beauty. Within a few miles we find Keiland Barton and Ellicomb, Knathorn and Rudge Rew. A group of villages are named Upcott, Nethercott, Southcott and Fiddlecott, not to mention Middlecott and Pennycotts. Why the last one is in the plural perhaps some reader can tell me. Not far away are Trinity Leigh and a village with a grim name—Loosebeare. **Lapford** village stands above the line on our right, the tall tower of its ancient church standing guard over the thatched group below. The railway is twisting and turning this way and that to follow the valley. River Taw has just joined us on the left and will accompany us all the way to Barnstaple Bay. Before reaching **Eggesford** we see an old church standing absolutely alone in a field, the waters of the Taw rushing but a few yards from the porch. Fishermen in our carriage will be gathering luggage and rods together, for here there is six miles of exciting salmon and trout fishing to be enjoyed. Little Dart River, another fisherman's paradise, crosses beneath us and flows into the Taw at a particularly beautiful part of the line. The hills rise 300 feet above our level on both sides, with our collection of rivers and streams, roads and the railway gathered together in the valley. Woods are alongside the line as we reach **South Molton Road**. River Taw is now on our right very close to the line, sometimes so close as to momentarily disappear beneath the train. We reach **Portsmouth Arms**, wooded hills towering above the train on our left, the Taw, now a wide river, running in water meadows by our side.

Speeds : This is a fast section of the line and 50 m.p.h. is usual as far as Portsmouth Arms. Sharp curves here reduce speed.

ATHERINGTON

Woods

meadows A.377

PORTSMOUTH ARMS 200¾

Quarry

Woods

600'

River Bray

350'

B.3226

6 MINUTES

LINE FALLS 1:500

4 MINUTES

KINGS NYMPTON 500'

BARNPOOL

SOUTH MOLTON ROAD 197¾

Mill Woods 100'

HORRIDGE MOOR 600'

LINE FALLS 1:150

5 MINUTES

CHULMLEIGH

Little Dart River

CHEDDON BARTON 600'

Woods 200'

Sow Mill 400'

EGGESFORD 193¾

Church 200'

Nethercott

CHAWLEIGH

500'

River Taw

550'

250'

Bowerthy Wood

5 MINUTES

LINE FALLS 1:315

300'

LAPFORD

400'

LAPFORD 190

NYMET ROWLAND

Factory Mill

River Dalch

300'

Quarry

Rudge Rew

4 MINUTES

LINE FALLS 1:110

MORCHARD BISHOP

farmland

Southcott

River Yeo

MORCHARD Rᴰ 187½

300'

450'

Knathorn Brook grazing land

meadows 350' 500'

2 MINUTES

COPPLESTONE 186

A377

CONTINUED FROM PAGE 28

31

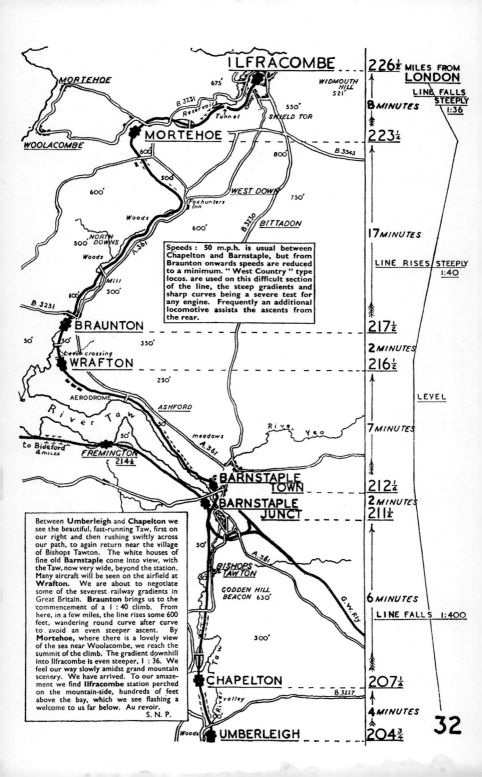

ILFRACOMBE — 226½ MILES FROM LONDON

LINE FALLS STEEPLY 1:36

8 MINUTES — 223¼

17 MINUTES

LINE RISES STEEPLY 1:40

Speeds : 50 m.p.h. is usual between Chapelton and Barnstaple, but from Braunton onwards speeds are reduced to a minimum. "West Country" type locos. are used on this difficult section of the line, the steep gradients and sharp curves being a severe test for any engine. Frequently an additional locomotive assists the ascents from the rear.

BRAUNTON — 217½

2 MINUTES

WRAFTON — 216½

LEVEL

7 MINUTES

FREMINGTON — 214½

BARNSTAPLE TOWN — 212¼

BARNSTAPLE JUNCT — 211½

2 MINUTES

6 MINUTES

LINE FALLS 1:400

Between **Umberleigh** and **Chapelton** we see the beautiful, fast-running Taw, first on our right and then rushing swiftly across our path, to again return near the village of Bishops Tawton. The white houses of fine old **Barnstaple** come into view, with the Taw, now very wide, beyond the station. Many aircraft will be seen on the airfield at **Wrafton**. We are about to negotiate some of the severest railway gradients in Great Britain. **Braunton** brings us to the commencement of a 1 : 40 climb. From here, in a few miles, the line rises some 600 feet, wandering round curve after curve to avoid an even steeper ascent. By **Mortehoe**, where there is a lovely view of the sea near Woolacombe, we reach the summit of the climb. The gradient downhill into Ilfracombe is even steeper, 1 : 36. We feel our way slowly amidst grand mountain scenery. We have arrived. To our amazement we find **Ilfracombe** station perched on the mountain-side, hundreds of feet above the bay, which we see flashing a welcome to us far below. Au revoir.
S. N. P.

CHAPELTON — 207¼

4 MINUTES

UMBERLEIGH — 204¾

32

'*Good Mornings*' begin with Gillette

Life and soul of the carriage, behold Mr. Gay who boasts that his blades make him bright for the day!

Blue Gillette blades **2/6** for **10** including Purchase Tax

A "WEST COUNTRY" ENGINE ON THE DIFFICULT MORTEHOE STRETCH NEAR ILFRACOMBE (SEE PAGE 32).

THE "ATLANTIC COAST EXPRESS" ON THE FAMOUS HONITON "BANK" (SEE PAGE 26).